# SOUL SIGHT

# SOUL SIGHT

### LEAD WITH VISION
### LIVE WITH INTENTION
### IMPACT WITH PURPOSE

## STELIOS NIKOLAKAKIS

**CoVerse**
COLLECTIVE

Published by Igniting Souls
PO Box 43, Powell, OH 43065
IgnitingSouls.com

LCCN: 2025910009
Paperback ISBN: 978-1-63680-514-6
Hardback ISBN: 978-1-63680-515-3
eBook ISBN: 978-1-63680-516-0

Available in paperback, hardcover, e-book, and audiobook.

Any Internet addresses (websites, blogs, etc.) and telephone numbers printed in this book are offered as a resource. They are not intended in any way to be or imply an endorsement by Igniting Souls, nor does Igniting Souls vouch for the content of these sites and numbers for the life of this book.

Some names and identifying details may have been changed to protect the privacy of individuals.

The superscript symbol IP listed throughout this book is known as the unique certification mark created and owned by Instant IP[IP]. Its use signifies that the corresponding expression (words, phrases, chart, graph, etc.) has been protected by Instant IP[IP] via smart contract. Instant IP[IP] is designed with the patented smart contract solution (US Patent: 11,928,748), which creates an immutable time-stamped first layer and fast layer identifying the moment in time an idea is filed on the blockchain. This solution can be used in defending intellectual property protection. Infringing upon the respective intellectual property, i.e., IP, is subject to and punishable in a court of law.

# DEDICATION

For my boys—Thomas, Michael, and Gabriel. You are my greatest teachers, my deepest why, and the clearest vision of love I will ever know.

# TABLE OF CONTENTS

# PART THREE: PURPOSE

# A NOTE TO THE READER

I didn't write this book for an audience. I wrote it for me.

Not the "me" you see on stages or in the clinic or on Zoom calls. The "me" who once sat alone outside an NICU, struggling to breathe. The "me" who held his son's hand in silence, trying to transmit strength through touch. The "me" who kept functioning on the outside while quietly unraveling within.

This book began as a means of survival. A way to give shape to pain I didn't know how to carry. To find words for what felt unspeakable. To carve out a path through uncertainty that nearly broke me.

And then, somewhere along the way, I realized—I wasn't the only one who needed this.

If you're a father navigating complexity . . .

If you're a high performer who feels stuck, despite all the wins . . .

If you're someone who looks like they have it all together—but inside, you're asking, "Is this it?"

Then this book is for you, too.

This is not a self-help book. It's a map back to the parts of you that got buried under pressure, perfectionism, or pain. A map back to your own frequency. A map back to what I call Soul Sight[IP].

You'll read stories of heartbreak, healing, and unexpected joy. You'll meet my family—not as symbols of resilience, but as real people who've lived through things no words can fully capture. You'll meet clients who've done the inner work and emerged clearer, softer, and braver than they ever imagined.

But mostly, you'll meet yourself.

Because that's what happens when we slow down long enough to really look. We remember. We feel. We choose again.

So before you turn the page, I'll ask you what I asked myself:

If you had three months left . . .

How would you live?

Who would you become?

That's where this book begins.

And where your next chapter might just unfold.

— Dr. Stelios Nikolakakis

# WHAT WOULD IT TAKE TO OPEN THE EYES OF YOUR SOUL?

Before we begin, I want you to truly consider that question I ended my note with:

*If you just found out you have three months to live, how would you spend it?*

Sit with that, not as a thought experiment, but as a doorway.

This isn't about fear. It's about presence, expression, intuition. It's about whether you are living in alignment with your soul's vision—or drifting from it.

Grab a pen and paper and write down what you would prioritize and who you would show up as. What would you say, do, or finally become?

Now pause and look at your list.

How many of those things are you already doing? What on that list have you delayed, buried, or ignored? And what would you stop doing instantly if you knew the clock was running out?

Let's be clear—this is not a book about death.

It's about your life—the life you haven't fully claimed yet, the life your soul remembers.

Keep your list close. We'll return to it throughout this book. And if you let yourself take this journey with open eyes and an open heart, don't be surprised if your answers shift—radically.

That shift is what Soul Sight is all about.

# WHERE IT BEGAN

". . . prep her for emergency C-section . . ."

That's all I heard before the doors slammed shut.

And suddenly, I was alone in a hospital hallway staring at the doors that separated me from my wife, Fabi, and my unborn twins, Michael and Gabriel.

Tears streamed. I had no idea what the hell was happening. Life was about to change, and fear consumed me.

Fear of the unknown.

Fear of being alone.

The day started with Fabiana calling out to me from downstairs. Twenty minutes later, we were at the hospital, bracing for the insecurity that went with what we already knew: one twin would be born sleeping. We weren't sure if the other would come that day or if he would even survive.

By the time they called for the emergency C-section, I was mentally and physically exhausted. But when those doors closed, something inside snapped. Every cell in my body went on high alert. I felt my breaths shorten and my chest tighten. Adrenaline burned through me.

When the doors leading to the operating room closed, they separated me from three out of the four people I love most in this world, and they became a symbol of the unknown. A line I couldn't see past, but one I had no choice but to cross.

I don't remember what happened with Michael. We knew six days before he wouldn't make it. There was no space for grief. I was in protector mode. All I saw was Fabi on the table with her insides on her chest, the surgeons moving fast, and Gabriel's resuscitation team prepping in the corner.

I know how to read a room, especially an operating room. Jokes and relaxed chatter signal things are fine. The dead silence and tense faces told me all I needed to know. I scanned every expression and flinch, ready to act if something went wrong.

They pulled Gabriel out and rushed him across the room. I locked on. *I will do whatever it takes to make sure he lives and that Fabi makes it too.*

They took Fabi to her room, but I stayed with Gabriel, watching him fight for every breath.

Wires surrounded my tiny son, and the medical team moved into action.

The fear inside tried to scream, but the protector in me was louder. I would not let the fear stop me. Not now. Not ever.

For the next 146 days, the NICU became our second home. I lived in fight-or-flight mode. Hyper-vigilant, I pretended to be strong while feeling like a ghost inside. We spent every night at home, terrified the phone would ring telling us we'd lost him.

There was no space for grief—only survival.

Those operating room doors became the metaphor for my life. Every time I've had to fight for Gabriel, with every unknown in my business, family, or faith, it's the same.

Doors closing.

Fear rising.

Adrenaline pumping, and me choosing to walk through anyway. That's who I am. I act in spite of fear, especially when what I value most is on the other side.

## THE GOLDEN BUDDHA

Years later, I came across the story of the Golden Buddha. As the story goes, monks covered a massive gold statue with layers of plaster and cement to make it less attractive to invading armies. Over time, people forgot what lay beneath, and for generations, people believed it was a simple clay statue.

Until the day they relocated the Buddha and the plaster cracked, revealing a glint of gold beneath the surface. It took that crack for the truth to be seen.

When I heard that story, I realized that was what was happening to me.

We all start like the Golden Buddha. Then life piles on fear, expectations, and disappointments like layers of plaster until we forget who we really are. We hide our gifts, our intuition, our potential.

It takes the cracks—the moments we fear will break us—to reveal the gold that has been there all along.

Those hospital doors created a crack. The fear, the heartbreak, the adrenaline, the uncertainty—it all broke something inside of me I could never put back.

Still, deep within, I sensed my adrenaline, fear, and overwhelming loneliness had roots as extensive as an oak tree, and the essence of who I am was hidden behind an emotional facade. I was a Golden Buddha and didn't fully know it.

Eventually, I realized the fear I felt wasn't meant to stop me. It was there to reveal me. It taught me that even in the chaos, we can find clarity. Even in darkness, we can find purpose. Even in fear, we can find the strength we didn't know existed.

That's what this book is all about—finding the gold beneath your cracks and walking through the doors you fear most. It's about learning to see your life through a new lens.

It's about gaining **Soul Sight**.

# PART ONE
## Paradox

# CHAPTER ONE
## FINDING GOLD IN THE MOST DIFFICULT SITUATIONS

Two years after Gabriel's birth, we received the diagnosis: quadriplegic spastic cerebral palsy with dystonia. I wasn't surprised. Deep down, I already knew. But hearing it aloud from a neurologist, with calm professionalism, carved the truth into memory.

Gabriel's chart mentioned atypical auditory neuropathy. Tests showed profound hearing loss—yet somehow, he responded to sound. The doctors were amazed. Was it a miracle? Or neuroplasticity at work?

That night, I didn't collapse into despair. I didn't surrender to the word 'impossible.' I knew, without explanation, that Gabriel would see, hear, speak, and even walk. There was a certainty in my bones I couldn't ignore.

A few weeks later, a trusted colleague visited. After observing Gabriel's posture, he gently offered an idea I hadn't considered: vision therapy. At first, I was stunned. What did vision have to do with cerebral palsy? I'd been practicing for fifteen years and never seen that connection.

But I didn't hesitate. If there was even a chance it could help, I was in. That's how transformation begins—when instinct overrides doubt. I dove into research and eventually traveled to study neurovisual development.

That's when everything changed. I discovered vision wasn't just about seeing—it was how the brain made meaning of what was seen. It was how the nervous system interprets the world. And little by little, that understanding began to shift everything for Gabriel.

We adjusted his lenses. We trained his brain to process sound differently. We watched his world begin to open. His eyes straightened. His hearing improved. The limitations the world assigned him began to dissolve.

At a follow-up visit, his ophthalmologist at Toronto's SickKids hospital looked up from her notes and said, 'I don't know what you're doing, but keep doing it.' I whispered inside: Yes.

That moment wasn't just a medical win—it was a crack in the old belief system. A glimpse into a new possibility.

## BIGGER THAN GABRIEL

Eventually, this expanded beyond Gabriel. At my clinic, we began screening children using the Developmental Eye Movement (DEM) test. We offered it for free. The results shocked us—25% of the kids had vision-related issues that impacted their reading and learning.

That data lit a fire in me. I could feel the mission growing. We rebranded the clinic, and I started coaching and training others. What started as a quest to help my son became a much bigger calling.

What I thought were the most painful cracks in my life—Michael's passing, Gabriel's diagnosis—became the very openings where light poured in. They revealed gold I didn't know I had: strength, purpose, vision.

At the time, I couldn't see it fully. But now I understand: this rupture—this complete dismantling of identity—was the first doorway.

It became the rebrand of my practice to what is now called *Mind's Eye Neuro-Visual Optometry*, where we support patients with learning disabilities, attention deficit disorders, concussion rehabilitation, and even high performers seeking sharper focus and clarity.

You see, when we stop resisting what breaks us and start asking what it reveals, something shifts.

That's when we move from surviving to living.

From fear to freedom.

From pain to Soul Sight.

# CHAPTER TWO
## GAINING SOUL SIGHT

Gabriel's diagnosis cracked something open inside of me. As I began to see the world differently—not just through my eyes, but through my soul—I started asking deeper questions.

Why did this happen?

What was I meant to learn from it?

And most importantly: How could I transform pain into power?

I'm not talking about bypassing grief or pretending to be strong. I'm talking about allowing pain to be a doorway. I began to realize that Soul Sight isn't something we're born with. It's something we earn—through presence, humility, and the willingness to see life through a new lens.

Gabriel became that lens for me. He wasn't a burden. He was a teacher. I never saw him as a child with a disability—I only saw him as perfect. From the beginning, I knew the situation itself was perfect too. Not easy. Not painless. But perfect in what it came to teach me.

Gabriel reflected back exactly what I needed to see in order to grow. Every day with him reminded me that life does not hand us mistakes, only lessons disguised as challenges.

## SILENCE THAT SPEAKS

There were days I felt lost, doubting everything, days I wanted to give up. Healing didn't come in a straight line; it came in spirals.

And yet, in those spirals, something began to shift. I realized that nothing in life happens to us. It happens for us. The cracks I resisted most were the very ones revealing gold I didn't know was hidden.

Soul Sight isn't about escaping pain. It's about letting pain shape us into people who can hold more love, more truth, and more light than before.

A Vipassana meditation retreat helped me see more light. For ten days, I sat in silence. No speaking. No eye contact. No distractions.

On the third day, my mind screamed. On the fifth, it softened. By the tenth, I wasn't just seeing differently—I was hearing myself again.

In the silence, memories rose. Vibrations coursed through my body. Tears streamed down my face. And then I heard Michael's voice:

*"Okay, Dad. Remember—you have three sons, not two."*

Another voice followed—the sister I never knew, telling me she was watching over me.

The stillness didn't erase my pain. But it gave me space to feel it fully, without needing to fix it. That was when I understood: pain is not the end of the road—it's a teacher, if we are willing to listen.

## VULNERABILITY AND PERSPECTIVE IN UNEXPECTED PLACES

The lesson continued in a place I least expected—in an environment completely opposite of Vipassana, a high-performance program filled with ambitious entrepreneurs called Strategic Coach˚.

On paper, it was about growth and strategy. But as I shared my story, the room shifted. People stopped planning and started feeling. We cried. We connected.

That's when I realized vulnerability is magnetic. It doesn't repel strength—it invites it. And it doesn't just belong in spiritual spaces. Soul Sight can show up in boardrooms, classrooms, even locker rooms—anywhere someone chooses to see through the lens of truth instead of performance.

At the beginning of my career, I thought my role as an optometrist was simply to help people see more clearly. But I discovered vision is much more than the mechanics of the eye. Vision is how the brain interprets what the eyes take in. It is the meaning we make of what we see. As Dan Sullivan, co-founder of Strategic Coach, puts it: "Our eyes only see and our ears only hear what our brain is looking for."

That's Soul Sight. Real vision is seeing your fear, your wounds, your past—not as punishments, but as invitations.

These cracks, these experiences—silence, vulnerability, perspective—they became the soil of something larger. I didn't know it then, but each crack planted a seed. And over time, I learned that these seeds were growing into a framework—a way of guiding others into the same clarity I had begun to discover. Strangely, that framework wouldn't emerge in a seminar or a clinic. It would come to life during one of the most uncertain seasons the world had ever known.

But even in those early days, I knew one thing for certain: my way of seeing was changing. And once you learn to see differently, nothing ever looks the same again.

# PART TWO
## PERCEPTION

# CHAPTER THREE
## INTRODUCING THE QUANTUM ACCESS METHOD

Sometimes a door opens when you least expect it. For me, that door opened during the strangest of times: a global pandemic.

COVID stripped the world to its bones. For many, it was a season of fear and isolation. For me, it became a crucible. The lack of usual noise forced me to face myself, and what remained was both unsettling and clarifying.

I spent years immersed in neuro-linguistic programming, hypnotherapy, and Timeline Therapy. Coaching others was meaningful, but it still felt incomplete. I didn't want to just coach. I wanted to help people transform themselves from the inside out.

## A Sacred Table

One quiet evening, I accepted an invitation to a Shabbos dinner. The table was simple, but the energy was palpable— sacred texts stacked nearby, laughter and stillness woven together, and conversations that touched something deeper than intellect.

What began as a meal became a nine-hour exchange about vision, healing, and human potential. It was the kind of dialogue that leaves an imprint—not because of the words, but because of the resonance you feel.

As I shared my work in vision and subconscious repatterning, I offered a simple Collier Gravitational Assessment—a test that reconnects the visual and nervous systems. The response was immediate and profound. Eyes softened. Nervous systems reset.

Something opened that night. Something subtle, but unmistakable.

Guiding the group through the earliest version of what would later become the **Quantum Access Method**$^{IP}$, I watched young leaders shift before my eyes. It wasn't just change—it was emergence.

That was when I knew: this wasn't just a method. It was a movement.

## INTEGRATION BECOMES INNOVATION

The Quantum Access Method developed as the integration of everything I had studied and lived—vision science, subconscious repatterning, energy psychology, and the wisdom carved by my own cracks.

It isn't about managing symptoms or fixing problems. It's about shifting perception at its root—bypassing logic and linear time to access transformation at the quantum level.

Why Quantum? Because just as quantum physics explores the unpredictable, non-linear behavior of matter, this work explores the unpredictable, non-linear layers of human consciousness. Transformation doesn't unfold step by step—it happens in leaps.

The Quantum Access Method is that leap.

Here's how it works:

- **S**urvey the Cracks—Pain isn't comfortable, but it will create those cracks that reveal the gold beneath.
- **I**nvestigate the Subconscious—When we don't understand where the pain originates, our subconscious sometimes holds the key.

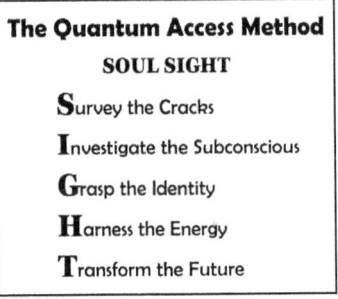

**The Quantum Access Method**
**SOUL SIGHT**

**S**urvey the Cracks

**I**nvestigate the Subconscious

**G**rasp the Identity

**H**arness the Energy

**T**ransform the Future

- **G**rasp the Identity—Reframing the past gives us the power to answer the question of "Who am I?".
- **H**arness the Energy—Learning to operate in the higher frequencies unlocks unimaginable power.
- **T**ransform the Future—Working through the Quantum Access Method opens the door to massive possibilities.

Soul SIGHT[IP] gives us Quantum Vision, allowing us to see beyond what we do and what we know into who we are, and tap into our Quantum Energy[IP].

## ENERGY AND FREQUENCY

At the core of this work is energy—the kind you feel when you're inspired, in prayer, in love, or in flow.

Our emotions act like a filter. They shape how we perceive the world. Low frequencies like fear, anger, and jealousy contract us, while higher frequencies like love, peace, and joy expand us.

Most of us live tethered to the lower frequencies, pulled by invisible cords of doubt and comparison. But those who learn to shift into higher states step into flow. They create differently. They live differently.

As Joe Dispenza says, "When you change your energy, you change your life." That is what the Quantum Access Method makes possible. It gives us access to those higher frequencies and brings change from the inside out. It gives us Soul Sight.

And Soul SIGHT releases Quantum Vision—the ability to see our patterns not as flaws, but as invitations to evolve. It reconnects us with the source that fuels all healing and expansion. That night around the Shabbos table, I didn't just watch a technique unfold. I witnessed people remember who they were.

The Quantum Access Method is more than a framework. It is a map that guides us back to the gold that was there all along. But that was only the beginning.

# CHAPTER FOUR
## VALUES LEVELS, EMOTIONAL BUNGEE CORDS, AND THE POWER OF CLARITY

I n the early days of coaching and optometry, I held some tools behind the curtain. I listened more than I spoke, quietly observing how people revealed themselves through their language, their frustrations, and the weight they carried.

What I noticed was this: we all have invisible tethers. I call them **emotional bungee cords**—attachments to old experiences that pull us back just when we're ready to leap forward.

On the surface, they look like procrastination, self-sabotage, or "hitting a wall." But beneath, it's something deeper: unhealed emotions lodged in the subconscious, waiting for us to notice. And when we see them, clarity begins to emerge.

## A MAP OF GROWTH

One of the most helpful maps I've ever discovered for understanding these patterns is Clare Graves' model of human development—what he called Values Levels.

It's not a hierarchy of "better" or "worse." It's a story of human awareness, showing how it naturally unfolds stage by stage. Each level carries its own gifts and limitations, and none should be discarded. We don't "graduate" and leave the earlier levels behind; we carry echoes of all of them within us, like rings in a tree trunk.

Here's a simplified sketch:

- **Level 1: Survival** – The first sign of level one is the newborn's cry. In Survival level, the body's primal demand for food, warmth, and safety takes control. Life is moment-by-moment. As we get older, trauma or hardship can pull us back here—paying bills, getting through the day, or simply breathing feels like the only focus.

  - *Example from daily life:* The college student skips meals because money ran out before payday.
  - *Leadership example:* A manager in crisis mode, trying to keep the company afloat, doesn't think beyond this week.

- **Level 2: Safety & Belonging** – We embrace our family or tribe. We begin to grasp family rituals, community traditions, and the first rules of "how we do things." Identity becomes rooted in belonging. When a toddler hears "No!" it lands as both reassurance—the world has rules—and wounding—life might be conditional. At this level, self-worth or the lack of self-worth begins to embed, and we learn what it means to be accepted and what it feels like to be abandoned.

  - *Example from daily life:* We go to church every Sunday because "that's what my family does."

- *Leadership Example:* A team clings to "the way we've always done it," resisting change to preserve harmony.

- **Level 3: Power** – We witness the fiery emergence of the individual. The "terrible twos" give us our first glimpse. Defiance, willpower, and raw ego energy grow. Later in life, this may show up as drive, ambition, or even aggression in the form of anger or rage. We see the primal insistence of *I matter, I exist, I will not be controlled.* It can feel messy, but it's a necessary step to individuation.

    - *Example from daily life:* A teenager slams the bedroom door, yelling, "You can't tell me what to do!"
    - *Leadership example:* The start-up founder, fueled by adrenaline and willpower, bulldozes others to prove himself.

- **Level 4: Order** – Structure enters. We embrace religion, school systems, law, and cultural codes. The "shoulds" and "musts" tell us how to behave and who to be. This level brings stability and shared meaning but can also limit self-expression. Many spend their entire lives here, measuring themselves against external systems and never questioning if those standards were truly chosen.

    - *Example from daily life:* We pay bills on time because "that's what responsible adults do."
    - *Leadership example:* A corporate manager prioritizes process over creativity and insists everyone "follow the handbook."

- **Level 5: Achievement** – Autonomy awakes along with the drive to build, achieve, and innovate. Entrepreneurs, visionaries, and leaders thrive here, fueled by ambition and possibilities. Many remain torn between levels four and five. They want freedom, yet fear, guilt, and old loyalties haunt them, tethering them to rules they no longer believe in.

  - *Example from daily life:* A person sets fitness goals and tracks them obsessively, taking pride in hitting every target.
  - *Leadership example:* A CEO focused on growth and expansion, celebrating innovation and restless for what's next.

- **Level 6: Connection** – This brings with it a conscious return to the collective; however, unlike Level 2, which was about safety in belonging, here the belonging is intentional and chosen. Compassion, justice, and empathy rise here. The focus shifts from "How do I win?" to "How do we rise together?" This level carries the energy of healing communities, activism, and shared humanity.

  - *Example from daily life:* A person volunteers at a food bank, not out of obligation, but out of genuine care.
  - *Leadership example:* A company prioritizes sustainability, equity, and culture alongside profit.

- **Level 7: Integration** – In this level, we have the ability to hold paradoxes. We can see patterns, complexity, and interconnectedness. Here, one doesn't reject the previous levels but integrates them. Contribution flows naturally, not from obligation or external approval, but from alignment with something far larger than self.

The power of this map lies in recognition. When we can see which level is speaking through us or through our colleagues, partners, or communities, then we can meet it with understanding instead of judgment. We stop fighting the stage we're in and start integrating the wisdom of each level into a fuller expression of who we are.

As you read this, notice:

- Where do you recognize yourself right now?
- Where do you recognize your parents, your team, your community?
- Where do you feel pulled forward—and where do cords pull you back?

## The Emotional Bungee Cords

Those emotional bungee cords are powerful.

They are the echoes of old fears, unmet needs, and protective strategies our younger selves created. They keep us tethered to earlier levels of growth, even when our spirit longs to expand.

An entrepreneur might dream of freedom but still hear a parent's voice of disapproval.

A parent might want to guide their child with love but unconsciously repeat patterns of shame.

A leader might reach outward with vision but inwardly still believe they're not enough.

The stronger the cord, the deeper the origin—and often, the bigger the gift it's guarding. That's the paradox: what feels like your heaviest burden may actually be the doorway to your greatest gift.

35

One young man in his late twenties came to me carrying these invisible cords. He didn't know it, but his life was being run by an early imprint of trauma—he had been physically abused at three years old, and while the memory was buried, the emotions never left.

They lived in his body as hurt, fear, insecurity, and defeat. They echoed through his relationships, his work, and his sense of self. Every time he tried to move forward, the cords snapped him back.

Through the Quantum Access Method, he began to see.

- Hurt transformed into *I am truth*.
- Insecurity shifted into *I am secure*.
- Fear dissolved into *I am safe*.
- Defeat reframed into *I am special. I am love. I am light.*

And with that shift, his values reordered themselves.

What had once been about insecurity and staying safe became about love, support, and inspiration. You could see the transformation not just in his words but in his body. His posture straightened. Tears of release became tears of joy. His vision—once clouded by doubt—shone with clarity.

And the result? His career flourished. His relationships deepened. Flow replaced friction.

The cords hadn't broken him. They had hidden the gold that was waiting all along.

## THE POWER OF CLARITY

We all carry these imprints. They're not mistakes. They're survival codes written in the language of the body. And until we bring them into awareness, they quietly govern us.

The invitation isn't to fight the cords. It's to see them. To understand them. To watch them loosen their grip.

This is where the Quantum Access Method performs its deepest work.

- By surveying the cracks, we discover the cords.
- By investigating the subconscious, we trace them back to their origin.
- By reclaiming identity, the cords no longer define us.

Clarity doesn't add more information. It clears the fog so what was always true can finally be seen. And when that happens—when the cord releases and the fog lifts—you don't just see differently. You are different.

## AN INVITATION

So let me ask you:

- Where are your cords?
- Where are you being pulled back into an old story?
- And what might happen if you saw those tethers not as failures, but as invitations?

Because here's the truth: we can only move as far as our vision allows us to see. And vision isn't just about the future—it's about understanding what shaped us, what's held us back, and what is waiting on the other side of fear.

That's where we're headed next: into the deepest layer of all—the unconscious mind.

# CHAPTER FIVE
## THE UNCONSCIOUS MIND

Values Levels give us a map that lets us see where we are and where we're heading. But what drives us—or keeps us circling the same loop—isn't just conscious choice. It's the unconscious mind.

It's astonishing how many of our invisible patterns live there—old memories, emotions, and imprints silently shaping how we see, act, and decide. We may be able to name the obvious events in our lives, but what we can't see, what lies beneath, holds even more power.

## THE BACKSTAGE CREW

From the time we're young, we're trained to value the conscious mind: analysis, reason, and logic. Yet no one teaches us how to partner with the unconscious—the backstage crew that quietly runs the entire production. The unconscious mind keeps us alive while we sleep. It heals our wounds without us thinking about it and stores every emotional imprint, whether we consciously remember it or not.

And when I began working with it directly, it was like the lights came on. Suddenly, I could see why so many of us feel stuck repeating old patterns.

I first learned about the prime directives of the unconscious mind in my NLP and Timeline Therapy training. It felt like language for something I'd always sensed.

1. **The First Prime Directive: Survival** – The unconscious keeps us breathing, our hearts beating, and our bodies healing. It's our most primal protector.

2. **The Second Prime Directive: Storage of Emotion and Memory** – It holds our earliest imprints of fear, anger, joy, or shame—even the ones we can't consciously recall. Sometimes it keeps them buried for decades, surfacing only when we're ready to grow.

3. **The Third Prime Directive: Fulfilling the Soul Contract** – Beyond protection, the unconscious also safeguards our gifts, purpose, and truth. Everything you're meant to become is already encoded within. The pain you feel? It's often just the wrapping paper. The gift is waiting inside.

## THE EMOTIONAL LENS

Every event in life gets filtered through this unconscious storage. To protect us, the brain doesn't just interpret what we see—it interprets whether it's safe to see it. Vision, therefore, is never just physical, it's also emotional. This is why people often lose memory of their earliest years, especially before age seven. Trauma, loss, or even unspoken family pain gets locked away. The unconscious hides it until the day we're ready to reframe it.

And here's something most of us never consider: the subconscious isn't only personal. It's generational as well. Science now shows that trauma can be passed down through **epigenetic mechanisms**. What your parents felt during pregnancy—their stress, grief, or joy—leaves an imprint. Unprocessed pain from ancestors shows up in descendants as fear, shame, or self-doubt. I lived this truth. My mother's miscarriage was never spoken of, yet the silence shaped me. Fear took root in me before I even had words for it. For years, I couldn't explain why I felt so alone—until I began this work and saw the generational threads.

## REFRAMING THE STORY

When Gabriel came home from the hospital, we lived in survival mode. There was no time or space to grieve Michael. We had to bury it for a time. But the unconscious doesn't erase; it waits. Eventually, the pain surfaced, demanding to be faced.

That's why **reframing** is everything. Without this new lens, we get stuck in the trauma. The Quantum Access Method guides people back to the root. Instead of getting stuck, we start to *see it differently.*

Take one client who found himself unexplainably trapped in fear. Therapists told him experiencing his father's death when he was five wasn't the issue. But when we uncovered that he hadn't been allowed to attend the funeral, everything clicked. His grief wasn't just about the loss—it was about being excluded from closure. When he reframed the story, he went from "I was abandoned" to "I am connected." The shift in his energy was instant.

Unaddressed, these old memories act like bungee cords. They tether us to stories that once kept us safe but now hold us back. Reframing cuts the cord. It doesn't erase the past. It transforms the meaning. Suddenly, the memory becomes less about what was done to us and more about what it's doing for us.

At first, freedom feels disorienting, like losing your footing. But that's just growth arriving. It's the nervous system re-learning what safety feels like without the tether.

## Healing Across Generations

I once worked with a woman who had survived kidnapping and torture. On the outside, she was a powerful advocate for women's rights. But she couldn't understand why she felt such an unstoppable drive.

When we explored, she realized her pain wasn't hers alone. She had inherited it—woven through generations of silence in her family. The moment she reframed that, her path took on new clarity. She understood she wasn't just healing herself; she was healing the line before her, and the line after her.

That's the ripple effect of reframing: when one person cuts the cord, the whole lineage breathes freer.

## Removing the Gestalt

Without reframing, the old story plays on repeat in the unconscious. It's like trying to answer an unsolvable equation. And each time we experience the emotion that the story evoked, it adds a block to our emotional pattern. We call the stack of blocks from that emotion a Gestalt. But when the lens flips, the entire Gestalt shifts—the whole emotional patterning dissolves.

Suddenly, the unconscious doesn't need to keep replaying the memory. Energy unblocks. Vision clears. And like Gabriel with his new lenses, the whole body begins to change.

## Your Turn

So I'll ask you:

- What memories feel heavier than they should?
- What patterns seem to repeat, no matter how much you try to "think" your way out?

- What if those aren't signs of failure, but invitations from your unconscious—reminders of the gold waiting beneath the cracks?

Your unconscious isn't trying to sabotage you. It's trying to protect you until you're ready. And when you're ready—when you allow yourself to see differently—the healing is not just yours. It radiates through generations. That is the power of the unconscious mind. And it's why the next step in this journey is learning how to truly shift your perspective.

# CHAPTER SIX

## THE CURRENT PERSPECTIVE

For as long as I can remember, I've wanted to help people see more clearly. At first, that meant restoring physical sight—fitting lenses, sharpening vision, working with the mechanics of the eye.

But over time, I realized clarity was never just about optics. Real vision comes from perspective. Our inner lens—our emotional wiring, our subconscious patterns, our inherited fears—shapes how we perceive the world and our place in it.

Everything I do is about vision. Whether I'm adjusting a lens, guiding someone through a breakthrough, or helping a parent reframe their past so they can show up more fully in the present—it's all connected. And the clearer I became about that truth, the more powerful the work became.

### START WITH THE BASICS

In Optometry, we always begin with a baseline exam—an exam that gives us a place to measure from before making any correction. Coaching works the same way. Before expanding someone's internal view, I first need to understand their current perspective.

I often begin with a question:

"Looking ahead one year, what needs to happen in your life for you to feel powerful, excited, and energized?"

Some pause and stumble over the answer. Others light up instantly, describing thriving kids, a growing business, and deepening relationships.

Their answers—or their silence—tell me everything. The way we envision the future reveals where we're seeing clearly and where it's foggy.

Once a vision emerges, I ask: "What's been in the way?"

At first, people blame money, time, or uncertainty. But when we dig deeper, we almost always find the same thing: emotional residue from the past still shaping the present.

## DANGERS, OPPORTUNITIES, STRENGTHS

Dan Sullivan created a concept called the D.O.S. Conversation‸, which invited us to name our biggest Dangers, our greatest Opportunities, and our strongest Strengths.

When people articulate their dangers—what they fear most—we can begin reframing them. And that's when confidence starts to grow.

This process reveals what I call the Current Vision Field^IP. It's not just what people want—it's how they see. Are they trapped in a reactive lens? Stuck in blind spots? Living out someone else's script? The Current Vision Field becomes the starting point as we map out the work ahead.

## WHAT'S HOLDING YOU BACK?

For me, fear was the biggest cord tethering me to the past. I later realized that fear wasn't just mine. It ran through my father's lineage. My grandfather survived war and instability. His nervous system was wired for vigilance. That vigilance passed through my father, and unknowingly, it lived in me.

Through reframing, I saw that fear wasn't a flaw—it was a function. It had protected my grandfather. It had protected my father. And for a time, it protected me. But once I understood it no longer served me, I transformed it.

"I am afraid" became "I am strong."

I see the same patterns in many entrepreneurs I work with. From the outside, they've built impressive success. Yet inside, something feels missing. They can't explain the anger, shame, or quiet fear holding them back. That's the unconscious mind at work—emotional cords still tugging them toward old patterns.

When we name the blocks, define core values, and sketch a future vision, the fog begins to lift. People start to see links between buried memories and the emotions shaping their present. And in that moment, the ability to choose returns.

## Holding Space for the Possible

I learned this lesson—the power of choosing what I allow to frame me—during one of the most fragile moments of my life.

When Fabi and I were waiting for Michael and Gabriel's birth, the doctor walked in with a list of warnings. The air grew heavy with the possibility of loss.

I covered Fabi's ears and turned to the doctor:

"Get out. We don't need that kind of energy right now."

Later, when the doctor asked if I had been angry, I told her, "Don't ever do that to another patient. Don't just give them protocols. Speak life. Speak vision."

Even in uncertainty, I chose to hold space for what was possible. And I've never stopped. For Gabriel. For my clients. For everyone who walks through my doors. Because when we hold space for possibility, we invite radiance, energy, and freedom.

## FLIPPING THE LENS WITH PURPOSE

This is what happens when perspective shifts:

- Pain becomes purpose.
- Fear becomes fuel.
- Vision becomes the map.

I don't want people to just feel better. I want them to see better—to see their past in context, their present with honesty, and their future with fire.

Most people don't even realize they're looking through a lens at all. That's why the first step in the Quantum Access Method is always this: **Survey the Cracks**. Because once we can see the filters, we can begin to shift them. And when we shift them, we don't just change how we see—we change how we live.

# Chapter Seven

## THE FIVE FIELDS OF VISION— A MAP I DIDN'T KNOW I WAS FOLLOWING

I n Gabriel's early years, I moved through life on instinct. Like many parents facing trauma, I went into autopilot—doing what needed to be done, pushing emotions aside, holding it together for everyone else.

Over time, through my own healing and the journeys of my clients, I began to notice a pattern. Everyone seemed to move through the same layers of perception—physiological, emotional, and energetic—on their way to regulation, clarity, and reconnection with themselves.

I felt this intuitively, but didn't know how to explain it until I began working closely with Dr. Angela Peddle. Angela introduced me to her *Five Fields of Vision*. At first, I viewed it as a helpful framework. But soon, I realized her model described exactly what I had already lived and everything I witnessed in others every day. She put language to what I'd been sensing for years.

Angela treated Gabriel with neuro-functional lenses that unlocked unexpected shifts in my son. She also guided me personally through vision therapy, helping me make sense of patterns I had stored not just in my mind, but in my body and visual system. The *Five Fields of Vision*, which Angela describes in her book *Becoming the Vision*, revealed to me that healing isn't just about eyesight. It's about how we live.

Looking back, I can see these Five Fields were the unseen coordinates of the work I was already developing through Quantum Access. What once felt purely intuitive now had structure—a map I didn't know I was following. They became the tool that lets us **Investigate the Subconcious**.

The Five Fields of Vision aren't abstract concepts. They're the architecture of how we perceive the world and experience ourselves. They show us how the nervous system organizes reality, both consciously and unconsciously. And most importantly, they give us a path to transformation.

## BODY VISION: THE FIELD OF SAFETY AND SURVIVAL

The foundation for the entire system is *Body Vision*. Our body tracks danger long before our mind catches on. Our posture stiffens. Breath shortens. Eyes scan but never settle. We hover in hyper-vigilance, and some completely shut down.

When Gabriel was born, I stopped feeling my body. My system went offline. I couldn't afford to collapse, so I didn't cry. It was years before I could sense and trust my body again. But when I did, everything began to shift.

I've seen this with countless clients. Chronic tension, fatigue, anxiety—all these things begin to ease when we restore safety to the nervous system. Safety isn't just a feeling. It's a field. And if we don't rebuild this one first, nothing else holds.

Ask yourself: *Can I feel my feet right now? Can I breathe fully into my belly? What does my posture say about my inner state?*

## Field of Focus: The Subconscious Gatekeeper

The Field of Focus governs what we notice and what we miss. While Body Vision centers on safety, Focus filters our reality.

During my most difficult seasons, my lens narrowed to urgency and crisis. My brain couldn't see softness or opportunity. It filtered out connection. Fear distorted my vision.

When we help clients restore their Field of Focus, their world opens. They stop scanning for danger and begin noticing choice, beauty, and opportunity.

Ask yourself: *What do I always notice first—what's wrong or what's working? What might I be missing because I'm not looking for it?*

## Field of Meaning: The Emotional Decoder

The Field of Meaning allows us to interpret experience and decide what it says about us. The interpretation is often more powerful than the event itself.

For years, I believed Gabriel's birth meant I had failed—that I hadn't protected him. I didn't consciously choose that belief, but it shaped my identity and decisions for years.

Meaning lives in the shadows until we bring it forward. Until we bring it into view, we keep reacting to things that don't seem logical. Only in the light can we see whether the story we're living is actually true.

Ask yourself: *What did I make that moment mean, and is it really true?*

## FIELD OF EXPRESSION: THE UNSPOKEN SELF

The Field of Expression is where our internal world becomes visible—through our voice, words, gaze, and gestures. Many of us learn to restrict this field early in our lives. We've been taught that some emotions are too much, too weak, or simply not allowed.

I carried this block myself. Outwardly, I was a communicator and a leader. Inwardly, I carried silence. Sadness, fear, even joy felt unsafe to voice.

Expression doesn't have to be loud or dramatic. It means congruence. What's happening on the inside matches what's being shared on the outside. When this field opens, people begin to speak truths they didn't know they carried. They feel real again.

Ask yourself: *Where do I hold back my truth? Who am I when I'm fully expressed?*

## INNER VISION: THE FIELD OF PURPOSE AND KNOWING

The final field is Inner Vision. This is the field of soul, identity, and the truth beneath all roles. When this field is clear, people feel a quiet sense of alignment. Choices feel right in the body. Approval seeking fades. They remember who they are.

In my own journey, it took years before I could finally say, *I feel like myself again.* But when it came, it wasn't triumph; It was softness. It was coming home.

Ask yourself: *Who am I beneath the story I've been living?*

The five fields sit at the core of how I now guide my clients. Whether we're doing subconscious work, vision therapy, or emotional release, everything flows through these layers. The flow isn't linear; the fields overlap and shift. But once you know they exist, you can begin to track your own healing.

Knowing this lets you understand why certain strategies don't work—they're aimed at the wrong field. You'll understand where you're stuck—not because you're broken, but because your system is protecting something deeper.

The Five Fields give us a language for what was once invisible. And they give us a path forward. One that's compassionate, integrated, and deeply human.

In the next chapter, we'll look at how these fields are shaped, often unconsciously, by inherited stories and emotional imprints. Because before we can change our lens, we first need to understand where it came from.

# CHAPTER EIGHT

## WHO AM I?

After we **Survey the Cracks** and **Investigate our Subconscious,** we can move on to **Grasp our Identity.** Now that we've explored the Five Fields of Vision—the architecture of how we perceive and process the world—we can taste freedom. But beneath the layers of those five fields lies a deeper question: *Who am I within them?*

You'd think this question would be easy. But most of us, myself included, answer with roles. "I'm a doctor." "I'm a parent." "I'm a spouse." Titles, credentials, and accomplishments define us because we haven't yet fully claimed the internal truth.

I didn't realize how much I leaned on those titles until a friend—a brilliant entrepreneur—looked me straight in the eye and said, "I would use you as my coach."

I blinked. "Me? Really? What about your guy?" I knew he was close to a renowned coach.

He shrugged. "He's too direct, too sharp. You're empathetic. You see me."

That moment cracked something open. It wasn't about my credentials. It was about presence and the energy I bring to the room. That's when I began to grasp the depth of my Unique Ability°, and with it, my true identity.

Because what we are is different from who we are.

Once you begin to regulate your body, focus your lens, reframe your meaning, open your expression, and trust your inner vision, the next step naturally emerges: Identity. This is where it gets personal fast. The question shifts from *What has happened to me?* to *Who am I becoming because of it?*

## THE "I AM" THAT FOLLOWS YOU

One of the clearest windows into identity is the story we tell ourselves. And it shows up most powerfully in the words we whisper after the phrase, "I am."

For years, my quiet *I am* statements were corrosive:

I am scared.

I am lonely.

I don't belong.

They weren't always conscious, but they shaped my energy, my choices, and my presence. When Gabriel was born, those thoughts screamed even louder.

But with each terrifying moment, I had a choice. Survive it, or reframe it.

I am scared. → I am courageous.

I am lonely. → I am deeply connected.

I don't belong. → I am a father, a guide, a soul anchored in love.

These reframes weren't affirmations scribbled on a whiteboard. They were forged in fire with oxygen tubes, sleepless nights, and decisions that shook me to the core.

This is how transformation unfolds:

- When you pray for embodiment, the Field of Body Vision doesn't soothe; it activates, disrupts, and reveals what's been frozen.

- When you seek clarity, the Field of Focus doesn't offer answers; it hands you distortion until you learn to filter truth.

- When you ask for self-worth, the Field of Meaning surfaces old stories until you reclaim the narrative.

- When you long to release the words and feelings, the Field of Expression shakes loose the stuck energy until your voice rings true.

- And when you hunger for deeper insight, the Field of Inner Vision doesn't map your route; it removes the maps so your soul becomes the compass.

Growth isn't given; it's invited. And every invitation stretches your edges until the deeper "I am" emerges.

## WHEN IDENTITY AND VALUES ALIGN

One of the most revealing moments in coaching comes when I ask someone to name their values. Then, through their stories and energy, we uncover which values are truly running the show.

Leaders may claim their top values are purpose and growth, but their daily choices reveal that control and status are in charge. This mismatch creates restlessness, burnout, and emptiness.

But when your values and identity align, when the *I am* matches the way we live, something remarkable happens.

Peace.

Power

Presence.

## REFRAME THE LABELS

Some of the heaviest chains we bear are the labels:

I am stupid.

I am broken.

I am a fraud.

But these aren't truths. These are stories, and stories can be rewritten.

That's what the Quantum Access Method makes possible—going back to the origin point of the belief and flipping the lens.

I am abandoned becomes I am strong.

I am hurt becomes I am powerful beyond measure.

The unconscious listens. It locks onto whatever follows *I am*. Which means identity is not about denial; it's about reclaiming the deeper truth that has always been there.

## RECLAIMING MY IDENTITY

When I went through the Unique Ability process with Julia Waller at Strategic Coach, I had to ask ten people I respected to reflect my gifts back to me. Their answers stunned me.

"You bring presence. You create a safe space. You connect soul-to-soul."

Julia asked, "Where does that come from?"

I didn't know at first. But then I realized—it's always been with me. It's a connection to what I now call Lifeforce Energy[IP]—an ability to bridge people back to themselves—to source, to truth. That's when I stopped seeing myself as a title or role. I am a guide, a bridge, a soul midwife.

And none of this would have been possible without facing the cracks or reframing the pain into purpose. If I hadn't chosen, again and again, to step through fear into truth, I could never have uncovered my *I am*.

Identity is not something we find; it's something we reclaim.

## IDENTITY MAP: THE DOOR TO BECOMING

If you want to step into your true "I am," here's the path:

1. **Notice your "I am" statements.** Write them down without judgment.
2. **Trace their origins.** Where did this identity come from?
3. **Flip the lens.** What deeper truth is trying to emerge?
4. **Align with your values.** Do your actions reflect your stated values—or your old stories?
5. **Reclaim your identity.** Beyond roles and titles, who are you at your core?

Grasping your identity doesn't mean you arrive. It means you finally begin. Because once you know who you are—not just what you are—the doors of possibility swing open wide. Now you're ready to step into the gift only you can bring: your Unique Ability.

# Chapter Nine
## THE FREEDOM OF SOUL SIGHT

While Gabriel was in the NICU those first few months, Fabiana needed to be with him round the clock. I stopped in every evening to sit with Gabe and speak to the doctors and nurses, but during the day, she took over.

This meant I spent more time than usual with our older son, Thomas. At first, I thought I was just keeping him busy, trying to distract both of us from the weight of what was happening in the hospital. But looking back, I realize how foundational those moments were.

Thomas and I created a tradition. Every Sunday, I took him to Canada's Wonderland, an amusement park in Toronto. Then we would visit Gabriel, grab hot dogs, and feed the pigeons. It was simple, sacred, and deeply bonding.

Brave for three, Thomas loved the roller coasters. As he grew, he looked forward to being tall enough to ride the next biggest coasters. Year after year, he measured himself against the height restriction signs in the park, asking, "Did I make the cut yet?"

## DON'T BE AFRAID OF THE RIDE

Years later, Gabe caught the roller coaster bug, too. He started on the smaller rides at Disney, but one summer at Canada's Wonderland, he was tall enough to ride the Leviathan— the biggest and fastest coaster in the park with its towering 306-foot first drop and high speeds up to 148 km/h.

He sounded so excited when he said, "Dad, I want to ride the Leviathan."

My heart stopped. I wasn't ready.

Gabriel is in a wheelchair. He has limited control over his limbs and core, and while his spirit is mighty, his body doesn't always cooperate. Immediately, I flashed back to those operating room doors. That same sickening uncertainty washed over me.

How would he hold himself in place? What if something went wrong?

"We have to make sure you fit in the demo seat," I said as I secretly hoped he wouldn't. Sure enough, he passed every test. The seat clicked shut, and the green light came on.

"Okay, Dad, I want to go."

My mind raced. I checked every seatbelt, every lock, every angle. I watched every staff member. I wanted someone— anyone—to say this wasn't safe.

Gabriel had just started to sound a little hesitant when Thomas joined us. But the older brother egged him on. "Come on, Gabe. I'll give you a hundred bucks if you ride!"

Gabe lit up with excitement and said "Game on, let's go!"

When our turn came, we locked him in. Thomas and I flanked him and locked arms with him. The ride launched, and I stopped breathing. I watched Gabriel's face the whole time—the joy, the thrill, the freedom.

This wasn't just a fun day at the park. This was a moment of impossible courage. For a child whose body has been through countless hospital stays, therapies, and surgeries, this was defiance in motion. Gabriel shouted to the world, *I'm not just surviving—I'm living.*

## THE ZIPLINE

A zipline high above Whistler, British Columbia, tested my trust again. I had arranged the experience for the whole family through a friend. He assured me it was safe for Gabriel, then ten years old. He did not tell me the first leg is 150 feet in the air, and Gabe would be going alone.

When we reached that first platform, I froze. Gabriel's diagnosis isn't just a label—it's a daily reality. Limited upper body control. Neurological unpredictability. Constant muscular tension. The idea of him flying solo across a canyon was unthinkable.

But not to Gabriel.

I was told I had to cross first to receive him on the other side. But thinking about Gabe crossing alone made me hesitate. Thomas looked at me with conviction and said. "Dad, go. I got this."

He did. So, I took off.

As I waited for him on the other side, Gabe zipped across flawlessly with a look of joy on his face that is impossible to describe. Then Thomas and Fabi followed.

For a child in a wheelchair to soar through the air unassisted is a miracle. But more than that—it's a message. It says, *Don't box me in. I will show you what's possible.*

## LIVING FULLY EXPRESSED

These moments—the roller coaster, the zipline—they're all portals. Each one cracks open our understanding of what it means to see clearly. Soul Sight is acting from purpose, not panic. It's breathing through the fear and choosing love anyway. It doesn't eliminate the unknown; it helps you trust it. And it invites you to live fully expressed. Because once you've seen life through this lens, once you've reframed your past and harnessed your energy, there's no going back.

That's the freedom of Soul Sight. What began as a father trying to save his son became the map I now use to guide others back to their own Soul Sight. This map now has a name—the Quantum Access Method. And it's not just mine—it's yours, too. If you're ready to return, the path is already opening.

## REFLECTION: YOUR SOUL SIGHT MOMENT

Soul Sight doesn't arrive in a single lightning bolt—it reveals itself in moments of trust, courage, and perspective shifts. Gabriel's roller coaster and zipline experiences were mine.

Take a few minutes and reflect on your own life:

1. **Recall a moment of fear** – a time you weren't sure you could handle what was in front of you.
2. **Name the breakthrough** – what did you learn, gain, or discover about yourself through that experience?
3. **Reframe it with Soul Sight** – complete this sentence: *"That moment didn't just happen to me. It happened for me, because it revealed _____."*

When you begin to see your life through this lens, you'll notice patterns. You'll start to recognize that every challenge carried a seed of clarity, and every fear was an invitation to live more fully expressed.

# PART THREE
## Purpose

# Chapter Ten

## HELPING THOSE WHO ALWAYS HELP OTHERS

Most people who find their way to me share one thing in common: they are helpers. They're the ones others rely on—parents, entrepreneurs, leaders, teachers, healers, caregivers, and coaches. The world leans on them because they show up strong, capable, and steady.

But here's the question I always ask: **Who supports those who always support others?**

Helpers rarely pause to ask that for themselves. They give and give until their body tenses, their relationships thin, or their soul whispers in the quiet hours, *Is this all there is?*

On the outside, they look unstoppable. On the inside, something is quietly unraveling. They may find themselves:

- Overworking, unable to switch off.
- Self-soothing with screens, alcohol, shopping, or chaos.
- Stuck in chronic fight-or-flight patterns.
- Feeling emotionally numb in their closest relationships.
- Haunted by the unrelenting voice that whispers, *You're still not enough.*

These patterns don't mean they're weak; they mean they've carried responsibility for so long that they've lost sight of their own needs. This is the paradox of the helper: they save everyone else while quietly running on empty.

## PAIN AS PORTAL

Helpers usually come to me believing they just need more discipline or a better schedule. But the truth is, they don't need another strategy. They need permission to stop, to feel, and to heal.

In our work, we don't spend years circling the problem. Instead, we go straight to the root—not to erase it, but to extract the gift.

Traditional approaches often see pain as a problem to solve. We see it as a portal. We don't ask, "Why are you like this?" We ask, "When did this start? How did it serve you? What deeper truth is waiting to be seen?" That single shift changes everything. Pain stops being the enemy and becomes the teacher.

## THE POWER OF A COLLABORATIVE HEALING TEAM

No helper can heal in isolation. That's why collaboration isn't just a value for me—it's a strategy for transformation. Our collective, known as *InVision*$^{IP}$, brings together practitioners with different specialties but a shared mission of helping the helpers rediscover Soul Sight.

- One team member anchors the **neuro-visual and limbic integration work**, using the Five Fields of Vision™ to restore safety and clarity.

- Others bring deep expertise in **subconscious repro-gramming, emotional release, and energetic realignment.**
- Together, we weave a whole-system approach that moves far beyond traditional talk therapy.

We don't ask clients to relive trauma. Instead, we guide them to transmute it gently, powerfully, and permanently. And when that shift happens, they **Harness the Energy** and inhabit a completely different frequency—one that is clearer, calmer, and more aligned with who they really are.

If you are someone who has carried others for years but secretly wonders *Who's helping me?,* this is your moment.

You are not broken. You are simply waiting to realign. And when you do, you'll become more than a helper. You'll start leading from presence, clarity, and purpose.

# Chapter Eleven
## HOW COLLABORATION CAN CHANGE YOUR PERSPECTIVE

Healing the helpers is where it all begins, but what happens when those helpers unite? When people who've done the inner work begin to build together, collaboration itself becomes a spiritual practice. And that's what **Transformed the Future** for me.

### Meeting Chad: A Collision with Purpose

I met Chad T. Jenkins at a Strategic Coach Free Zone® event in Chicago. From the moment Chad heard about my work, he leaned in—not with polite nods, but with genuine curiosity and vision. We shared frameworks, pushed each other's thinking, reframed, restructured, and expanded. And out of that came not only a new friendship, but a movement.

One conversation with Chad shifted me forever. He asked about Gabriel's first Special Olympics. "On a scale of one to ten, what's this experience going to be like for you?"

"A ten for sure!"

"Perfect," Chad said. "Add a zero."

At first, I laughed. But I couldn't get his challenge out of my head. How could I make Gabe's Special Olympics a 100 out of 10?

Finally, I called my father. That Wednesday, three generations stood together—my dad, my sons, and myself—watching Gabriel race in front of 1000 screaming fans cheering him on towards that finish line.

It wasn't just a ten out of ten. It was a thousand out of ten.

That's what collaborations do. They multiply possibility exponentially.

## Thomas: A Leader in the Making

Collaboration doesn't happen only in boardrooms. It happens around kitchen tables and late-night conversations. My oldest son is living proof.

Thomas grew up in the gravitational pull of complexity. He had a childhood full of love, yes, but also filled with hospitals, Gabriel's medical challenges, and hard truths. From an early age, he understood something many adults never figure out: leadership begins with presence.

When he launched his first entrepreneurial project as a teen, he did it with clarity and heart. Thomas is more than a son; he's a quiet North Star. If Gabriel taught us courage, Thomas reminds us of grace.

## Creation Requires Collaboration

Too many believe collaboration is merely the exchange of resources. But true collaboration requires Soul Sight. It's not about me or you; it's about us and what we become.

When you understand yourself on a deeper level, you can connect more deeply with others, share ideas openly, and create something that didn't exist before.

Chad sees this better than most. He says creation has always been and will always be a collaboration. He understands the ideal way for me to bring something new to life is to join my best ideas with someone else's best ideas.

So, he and I joined our gifts for reframing:

- I reframe emotions and past trauma so people can create a compelling vision.
- Chad reframes friction, turning resistance into fuel for growth.
- Together, we lead *CoVision*$^{IP}$, a movement where entrepreneurs expand—they move from survival into legacy.

We don't run from friction; we mine it.
We don't avoid different perspectives; we invite them.
Because the future isn't built alone; it's co-created.

## THE THREE SHIFTS OF SOUL-ALIGNED COLLABORATION

Here's how you can begin to collaborate differently in your own life:

- **From Exchange to Expansion** – Don't stop at trading support. Ask: *What can we create together that neither of us could create alone?*
- **From Fear to Trust** – Friction isn't failure. It's fuel. Lean in. The breakthrough often hides inside the tension.
- **From Me to We** – Instead of asking, *What can I gain?* ask, *What can we build that serves beyond ourselves?*

Collaboration, at its core, is vision multiplied.

And when helpers unite—when people who've reclaimed their Soul Sight choose to co-create—the possibilities expand beyond imagination.

# CHAPTER TWELVE
## GIVING BACK

S oul Sight doesn't end with discovering your purpose. That's just the beginning. Once you truly see yourself, your story, and your power, you begin to see others. You move from what was done TO you, to what was done FOR you, to what can be done THROUGH you.

## MY OWN GIVING JOURNEY

My parents deeply instilled the ideal of contributing. Every December, my mother would hand my brother and me five dollars each to buy toys—not for us, but for the children at Toronto's SickKids hospital.

I loved the ritual, but I always wondered, *Who actually gets these toys?*

By high school, my friend Harry joined me, and we got bold. We took the toys straight to the oncology floor and handed them out room to room. One year, I handed a Barbie˙ to a girl who hadn't spoken since her diagnosis of cancer. When she whispered, "Thank you," her mom and nurse started to cry. I will never forget that moment.

Years later, when Gabriel was still in intensive care, a nurse stopped in his room and handed Fabi coupons that would allow us to pick out toys for our boys. When she returned, she was crying. "I have the answer to your question about who got your toys all those years ago. They're not just giving toys to kids. They're giving them to parents so they can feel like they remembered their kids on Christmas."

My childhood tradition had come full circle.

## THE POWER OF YOUR STORY

Much of Soul Sight is uncovering needs you didn't even know you had. When you embrace those hidden needs, you grow—and then you begin to anticipate the needs of others.

That's the ripple effect.

One of the most powerful aspects of the Quantum Access Method is that it allows people to own their story without being owned by it, and it frees them to give.

Giving back doesn't always mean grand gestures. Sometimes, it's choosing to be fully present with someone who's hurting. Other times, it's telling your story so someone else feels less alone. Often, it's modeling love when the old pattern was to shut down.

We don't just heal to feel better. We heal so we can give better, love better, and lead better.

## GABRIEL'S VOICE

Each of my sons has his own way of giving. Thomas leads with vision and service. Michael offers subtle winks from above. And Gabriel—though they once told us he would never speak—has become a global ambassador for people with disabilities.

On stage one day, he looked out at the audience and said, "Many times, people tell me what I cannot do, and I'm sure people sometimes discourage you, too, when you're doing something you really want. But don't give up. Keep trying. Find more courage and believe in your dreams and yourself. This way, we all feel empowered to do anything."

That's Soul Sight. We heal so others can rise.

# Chapter Thirteen

## THE QUANTUM ACCESS METHOD—A MAP TO YOUR INNER VISION

B y now, you've walked with me through heartbreak and healing. You've seen fear become a doorway, identity reclaimed, and vision expanded. What began as a desperate search for healing for my family has since become a framework for transformation: the Quantum Access Method.

Quantum Access isn't therapy or typical coaching. It is a fully integrated system designed to work across the subconscious, the somatic, the spiritual, and the energetic layers of your being.

At its core, Quantum Access is about alignment:

- Aligning your nervous system with your purpose.
- Aligning your internal story with your external reality.
- Aligning who you think you are with who you truly are.

# THE THREE MOVEMENTS OF QUANTUM ACCESS

1. **Discovery: Survey the Cracks**

   We begin by mapping where you are. What patterns keep snapping you back to the past? What blind spots fog your vision? Tools like the R-Factor® Question, Dan Sullivan's D.O.S.® Framework, and Values Levels help us bring the cracks into view.

2. **Integration: Investigate the Subconscious—Reframe and Regulate**

   Next, we go beneath the surface into the subconscious and the nervous system. Using NLP, Timeline Therapy, hypnosis, and neuro-visual tools like syntonics and balancing lenses, we revisit origin points. We don't rehash trauma; we reframe it.

   • I was abandoned becomes I am resilient.

   • I am broken becomes I survived, and now I thrive.

   • When the nervous system feels safe, the soul emerges.

3. **Transformation: Grasp Identity, Harness Energy, and Transform the Truth**

   Finally, we rewrite the story behind *I am*. Because whatever follows *I am* follows you. With identity reclaimed and energy aligned, people don't just heal; they transform. They step into presence, contribution, and purpose.

The framework of the Quantum Access Method changed everything—for me, my clients, their families, and the founders who now lead from Soul Sight. We don't process pain just to process it. We extract the gift, reclaim the soul, and activate the future.

Because when you bring the unconscious into awareness . . .

When you align the nervous system with love . . .

When you reframe the past and reclaim your truth . . .

**Everything changes.**

## The Invitation

If something stirred within you while you read, it wasn't an accident. It is resonance. And it's the first crack in the clay.

The map is here.

The door is open.

One question remains:

**Will you walk through?**

# AFTERWORD

## COMING FULL CIRCLE—
## IF YOU HAD THREE MONTHS

When Gabriel was born, I thought the story was about survival. Every day felt like a battle against fear, uncertainty, and limits. What I couldn't see then was that survival was only the beginning.

Through his courage, his laughter, and his determination to ride roller coasters and fly down ziplines, Gabriel taught me what true vision really is. It isn't about perfect circumstances. It isn't about the absence of pain. It's about seeing possibilities where others see walls.

Looking back, I see that Soul SIGHT was always there—hidden beneath layers of fear and expectations. It took pain to reframe purpose. It took collaboration and community to bring the vision to life. And now, it belongs not just to me, but to you.

If you've read this far, you've already begun the journey. You've surveyed your cracks. You've glimpsed your Golden Buddha beneath the clay. You've felt the invitation to reclaim your own "I am."

At the start, I asked you, "What if you had just three months left?"

Now, we return to that question. Look again at the people you name, the priorities you wrote, the noise you wanted to silence. Ask yourself:

- What would I do differently—starting today?
- How has my purpose evolved?
- What am I now truly ready to begin?

Because Soul Sight isn't about someday, it's about now. The gift of sight is the gift of presence—to notice not just what is before you, but who you are becoming through it. And when you live from that place—eyes open, heart awake, spirit aligned—you discover that the timeline never really mattered.

So I leave you with this:

May you hold your life gently.

May you walk with courage and compassion.

May you see the cracks as openings, and the gold as your birthright.

And may you live every day as if the three months you imagined begin now.

With filotimo and gratitude[IP],

Dr. Nik

# ACKNOWLEDGMENTS

This book was born from the deepest places of my heart—shaped by pain, clarity, and grace. But it could never have come to life without those who stood with me, challenged me, and reminded me what was possible.

To my boys—Thomas, Gabriel, and Michael—you are the heartbeat of this journey. Thomas, your quiet strength grounds this family. Gabriel, your courage teaches me daily what true freedom looks like. And Michael, your presence reminds me that love always finds its way. You are my why.

To my parents—thank you for every sacrifice, every lesson, and every possibility you gave me.

To Dr. Angela Peddle, Chad Jenkins, and James Prince—thank you for seeing the vision before it was fully formed and for bringing your genius to its unfolding. You are part of the very architecture of the Quantum Access Method.

To my "Bag Brothers," Areef Nurani and Vitu Banh—your loyalty, honesty, and belief carried me. You've been sounding boards, mirrors, and anchors.

To Moshe Mandelbaum, Binyomin Posen, and Demetri Zissopoulos—you believed in this work before the world had language for it. Around that Shabbos table in the middle of Covid, you reminded me it mattered and could reach farther than I ever imagined. Your encouragement helped launch "Dr. Nik," and your belief still fuels me today.

To my team at Mind's Eye—what you do each day changes lives. You bring light into vision and vision into life. Thank you for holding the frequency.

To my closest friends, colleagues, and vision therapy family—your prayers, presence, and faith in this work carried me more than you know. Thank you for being there when it mattered most.

To the mentors who shaped me—Dr. Bob Sanet, Dr. Rob Lewis, Dr. Nancy Torgerson, Dr. Paul Harris, Stefan Collier, Pilar Vergara, and Dr. Richard Kimbrough—your brilliance and generosity echo through this work. And to my early teachers—Mr. Hughes, Mr. Allen, Mr. Gillan—and every coach who saw more in me than I saw in myself: you planted seeds that still grow today.

To Fabiana—thank you for the years we shared, the growth we experienced, and the family we built together. This journey changed us both, and I'll always carry that with gratitude.

And to you, the reader—thank you for walking this path with me. If something in these pages sparked your heart, it's because the spark was already within you.

# ABOUT STELIOS NIKOLAKAKIS

A visionary leader and innovator in personal and professional transformation, Dr. Stelios Nikolakakis is driven by a passion to empower entrepreneurs, leaders, and change-makers. He developed a groundbreaking framework that blends spiritual insight with scientific rigor to create meaningful, lasting change.

As a Neuro-Visual Optometrist, Dr. Nikolakakis is dedicated to his expanding practice, and he's proud to be the leader of the Mind's Eye team, an exceptional group of professionals committed to improving the visual systems and daily lives of the patients at Mind's Eye Neuro-Visual Optometry.

Renowned for his expertise in leadership and personal growth, Dr. Nik combines the wisdom of ancient philosophies with modern psychology to deliver holistic and transformative experiences. His signature methods—Soul SIGHT and the Quantum Access Method—guide individuals toward profound paradigm shifts, deeper self-awareness, and alignment with their values and vision.

Stelios' extensive credentials include certifications as a Hypnotherapy Instructor, Registered Hypnotherapist, Neuro-Linguistic Programming Trainer, and Time Line Therapy Master Practitioner. Additionally, he earned a Doctor of Optometry degree and a Bachelor of Science degree from the University of Waterloo, showcasing his commitment to excellence in both scientific and human development.

Stelios makes his home in Toronto, Canada, where family remains at the heart of everything he does. His three sons, Thomas, Gabriel, and Michael, anchor his life's mission, reminding him daily of the values of love, vision, and legacy. Whether with his family or leading the Dr. Nik or the Mind's Eye teams, Stelios dedicates every moment to transforming all realms of vision for the better.

# Successful. Unfulfilled. Ready for more?

CoVISION™ is a transformational experience designed for high-achieving entrepreneurs who feel stuck, misaligned, or on the edge of a new chapter.

**The missing pieces:**
- Deep clarity on what's been blocking you
- A renewed sense of purpose and direction
- Clarity of a strategic path forward

**Unlock the shift. Map the way forward. Source tangible momentum from deep alignment.**

 Scan the QR Code or visit the website below to learn more.

**WWW.DRNIK.CA/COVISION**

# DR. NIK™

BE WITH PURPOSE

## Ready to break through
## the patterns holding you back?

Whether you're navigating burnout, a major life shift, or simply seeking more alignment, discover what's possible when you lead with clarity, confidence, and purpose.

**GET STARTED AT**
www.drnik.ca

# THIS BOOK IS PROTECTED INTELLECTUAL PROPERTY

## Instant IP <sup>IP</sup>

The author of this book values Intellectual Property. The book you just read is protected by Instant IP<sup>IP</sup>, a proprietary process, which integrates blockchain technology giving Intellectual Property "Global Protection." By creating a "Time-Stamped" smart contract that can never be tampered with or changed, we establish "First Use" that tracks back to the author.

Instant IP <sup>IP</sup> functions much like a Pre-Patent since it provides an immutable "First Use" of the Intellectual Property. This is achieved through our proprietary process of leveraging blockchain technology and smart contracts. As a result, proving "First Use" is simple through a global and verifiable smart contract. By protecting intellectual property with blockchain technology and smart contracts, we establish a "First to File" event.

Protected by Instant IP <sup>IP</sup>

# LEARN MORE AT INSTANTIP.TODAY